FAMOUS
LAST WORDS

FAMOUS LAST WORDS

FOND
FAREWELLS

DEATHBED
DIATRIBES

AND

EXCLAMATIONS
UPON EXPIRATION

COMPILED BY
RAY ROBINSON

PRINTED BY

WORKMAN PUBLISHING

NEW YORK

Published simultaneously in Canada by
Thomas Allen & Son, Limited.

Library of Congress Cataloging-in Publication Data
Famous last words, fond farewells, deathbed diatribes,
and exclamations upon expiration /
[compiled] by Ray Robinson.
p. cm.
ISBN-13: 978-0-7611-2609-6
1. Last Words. I. Robonson, Ray, 1920 Dec. 4-

PN6328.L3F366 2003

082—dc21   2003041057

ISBN-13: 978-0-7611-2609-6

Workman books are available at special discounts
when purchased in bulk for premiums and
sales promotions as well as for fund-raising or
educational use. Special editions or book excerpts can
also be created to specification. For details, contact
the Special Sales Director at the address below.

Workman Publishing Company, Inc.
225 Varick Street, 9th Floor
New York, NY 10014
www.workman.com

Printed in China

First printing April 2003

10 9

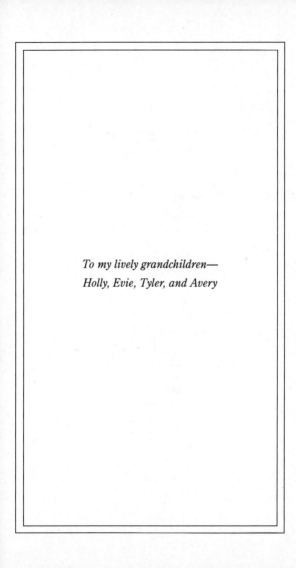

To my lively grandchildren—
Holly, Evie, Tyler, and Avery

INTRODUCTION

When my father, a New York City lawyer for over 45 years, died in 1957, he left behind a sterling reputation, but not much of material value. When I opened the large, black safe in his Midtown office, I discovered only an empty Coca-Cola bottle, a pair of tattered long underwear, and a tiny slip of white stationery. Scrawled on the paper in my father's hand were the words of a poem written in 1820 by Fitz-Greene Halleck, a banker, on the death of American poet Joseph Rodman Drake:

> *Green be the turf above thee,*
> *Friend of my better days!*
> *None knew thee but to love thee,*
> *None knew thee but to praise.*

For many years I carried Halleck's tribute to his friend in my wallet (I discovered only later that it was in *Bartlett's Familiar Quotations*). I had never judged my father to be such a sentimental fellow. Yes, he devoured Shakespeare and had a lifelong passion for Columbia University football games and books about snakes, but for him to have cherished these four lines of poetry was another matter.

In time, as a result of finding that scrap of stationery, I began to collect farewell utterances from people in all walks of life. It became a pleasant obsession, although some consider it a morbid pastime. I dipped into new and old biographies, especially the final chapters where, inevitably, the subject would say something memorable or forgettable while reposing on his deathbed. I scoured newspaper "agony columns"—Sherlock Holmes's phrase to describe obituary notices in *The London Times*—and I listened eagerly to anecdotes told by friends and acquaintances. Along the way, lawyer Clarence Darrow's schadenfreude provided unintended encouragement: "I have never killed anybody, but I have read many obituaries with delight!"

In the course of my research, it became clear that most of us have an interest not only in death, but in how we confront our last moments on earth—if, of course, we are sufficiently prescient to believe we are taking our last breaths. The subject is a grave one, yet I learned quickly that not all dying people treat the matter with gravity. In fact, this book contains a fair number of excellent one-liners. Besides the funny, though, you'll also find the mawkish, the panicky, the sad, mean, poignant, outrageous, and occasionally the incomprehensible. The beauty of some of these last words is that they may open a window through which we feel we can catch a glimpse, if only for a moment, of the entire life that preceded it.

I've come to appreciate the difficulty of authenticating so-called exit lines, since witnesses are often too distraught or confused to remember things accurately, or simply choose to edit or improve the remarks for the sake of posterity. Back in 1920, the dying Notre Dame halfback George Gipp is supposed to have murmured to football coach Knute Rockne, "Tell them to go out and win one for the Gipper." But it's not clear that Rockne was actually there at the time, and, moreover, Gipp was never known to his buddies, or anybody else, as the Gipper.

It is also true that reports of final utterances can vary. The adventurous Wilson Mizner is reported to have said to a priest just before he died, "Why should I talk to you? I've just been talking to your boss." Rival observers report an alternative quote: "Well, Doc, I guess this is the main event." Obviously, this material is not easy to document, but I like to think that the majority of the famous last utterances in this volume were uttered, in pretty much these words, shortly before the utterer's death.

So here they are, the parting words of poets, philosophers, athletes, scoundrels, politicians, gangsters, movie stars, lawyers, soldiers, pilots, tycoons, and the condemned, plus a handful of epitaphs and eulogies—not strictly last words, I know, but too good to pass up.

—*Ray Robinson*

"I've never felt better."

DOUGLAS FAIRBANKS

After suffering a heart attack in 1939 at the age of 57, "The King of Silent Hollywood" *(Robin Hood, The Thief of Baghdad, The Mark of Zorro)* reassured an attendant while resting at home, then went back to sleep and died that night. Fairbanks was an athletic movie star known for his charm, good looks, and—apparently—an inability to gauge his physical condition.

"I wish I had drunk more champagne."

JOHN MAYNARD KEYNES

The British Keynes was not your average economist. Keynes, whose eponymous theories influenced Roosevelt's New Deal and the rise of the European welfare state, was also a member of the famously liberated Bloomsbury group. He was politically liberal and sexually liberated, sleeping with many of the bohemian men in his circle and, of course, drinking champagne. Of that, and government spending, Keynes thought there could never be enough.

"It's very beautiful over there."

THOMAS EDISON

The Wizard of Menlo Park, arguably America's foremost inventor, received only three months of schooling in his entire childhood. Plagued by lifelong and worsening hearing loss, Edison's gifts to the world were more sound (the phonograph and talking movies), more light (the light bulb), and better communication (the telegraph). Near death in 1931, his second wife, Mina, asked him if he was suffering. "No," Edison replied. "Just waiting." Then he looked out his bedroom window and uttered his last words.

"You will show my head to the people— it is worth seeing."

GEORGES JACQUES DANTON

Shortly after giving these instructions to his executioner in 1794, the head in question was removed from Danton's body by guillotine. During the French Revolution, Danton was a Parisian lawyer who decried the Reign of Terror, which charged him with conspiracy to overthrow the government and then sentenced him to death.

"This is a sharp medicine, but a sure remedy for all evils."

SIR WALTER RALEIGH

Poet, explorer, and sometime-pirate Sir Walter Raleigh was a loose cannon in the English court. After his attack on a Spanish camp in South America almost started a war, England's peace-loving king, James I, sent for the headsman. Yet even people who didn't like Raleigh had to admire the clever exit line he tossed off from the scaffold.

"I would rather be a servant in the house of the Lord than sit in the seat of the mighty."

ALBEN W. BARKLEY

B arkley got his wish when, while quoting the Bible before a mock convention in 1956, he died of a heart attack. Admired for his story-telling and oratory, the 77-year-old Kentuckian served the Democratic party for 44 years as a congressman, Senate majority leader, and as vice president under Harry Truman.

"How were the circus receipts in Madison Square Garden?"

P. T. BARNUM

Entertainment and flummery were Barnum's business to the very end. During his brilliant career as a showman and shameless bunko artist, P. T. Barnum bamboozled the public into believing that half of a stuffed monkey sewn onto a fish tail was a mermaid, and that an elderly black woman was George Washington's 161-year-old nurse. He later billed his three-ring circus as "The Greatest Show on Earth."

"Please know that I
am quite aware of the
hazards. I want to do
it because I want to
do it. Women must try
to do things as men
have tried. When they
fail, their failure must
be but a challenge to
others."

AMELIA EARHART

Earhart knew as a teenager that she wanted to fly, and fly she did, setting dozens of records for both women and aviators of either sex. While attempting to circle the globe at the equator in 1937, she disappeared in the central Pacific and was never heard from again. Theories about her fate have ranged from her being sent to spy on the Japanese to becoming a South Pacific fisherman. Before taking off for the last time, she wrote this farewell letter to her husband, publisher G.P. Putnam.

"Mom, do you hear
the rain? Do you hear
the rain? Mom,
I just want to take off
in the plane."

JESSICA DUBROFF

Jessica's parents believed she was so special
that she would set a record as the youngest
person to fly east across the United States
at the age of seven. In 1996, after only four
months of flight training, she got as far as
Cheyenne, Wyoming, where she spoke her last
words over the phone to her mother shortly
before leaving on the next leg of her journey.

"Tell my mother I died
for my country.
I thought I did it for
the best. Useless,
useless . . ."

JOHN WILKES BOOTH

T he actor hailed a few years earlier as the
"youngest tragedian in the world" was
responsible for one of America's great tragedies.
After the 27-year-old Booth—rabidly pro-slavery
and quite possibly a Confederate spy—assassinated President Lincoln on April 14, 1865, he
fled to Virginia, where he refused to surrender
and was shot in the neck in a burning barn.

"My story is a love story, but only those who are tortured by love can understand what I mean. I was pictured as a fat, unfeeling woman. True, I am fat, but if that is a crime, how many of my sex are guilty? I am not unfeeling, stupid or moronic. My last words and my last thoughts are: Let him who is without sin cast the first stone."

MARTHA BECK

I f the 233-pound Martha Beck and her lover, Raymond Fernandez, had committed their crimes today, they would be guests on *Jerry Springer*. In the summer of 1949, American tabloids indulged the public's fascination with the trial of the "Lonely Hearts Killers," who had used personal ads to con and murder lonely women. Beck's lurid testimony and fleshy physique kept her on the front page, but just before her 1951 execution, she seemed to bite the media hand that had fed her.

"If you will send for a doctor, I will see him now."

EMILY JANE BRONTË

But it was too late to save the 30-year-old poet and author of *Wuthering Heights* from the final stages of tuberculosis. The stubborn and strong-willed Brontë refused medical help until the very end, and became the first ill-fated Brontë sister to die an untimely death.

"Am I dying or is this my birthday?"

LADY ASTOR

A s she lay dying at 85, the wealthy socialist and first female member of the
British House of Commons awoke to find
herself surrounded by her entire family. She
pondered the possible explanations for the
gathering with the same acid wit that had
immortalized her verbal sparring matches
with Winston Churchill. A passionate advo-
cate of women's rights, Astor spoke for her
entire sex when she declared: "We are not
asking for superiority for we have always had
that; all we ask is equality."

"Nothing so infuriates me as
the incapacity of seemingly
intelligent people to get it
through their heads that
God alone doesn't go
around this world with his
finger on the triggers, his
fist on knives, his hands on
steering wheels. . . . Never
do we know enough to say
that a death was the will
of God. . . . My own
consolation lies in knowing
that . . . when the waves
closed over the sinking car,

God's heart was the first of
all our hearts to break."

WILLIAM SLOANE COFFIN
in a eulogy for his son Alex

T he Reverend William Sloane Coffin,
former chaplain at Yale and senior minister of New York's Riverside Church, was an
early protester against racial segregation and
America's involvement in Vietnam. His elo-
quence was never more evident than at the
memorial service for his son Alex, who died
in an automobile accident in 1983, at the age
of 24.

"I were miserable if I might not die . . . Thy kingdom come, Thy will be done."

JOHN DONNE

In one of his Holy Sonnets, poet John Donne wrote that death was nothing more than a short sleep before eternal life. Born Catholic, Donne took Anglican orders in 1615, and went on to become one of the great theatrical preachers of his day. He delivered his own funeral sermon, "Death's Duel," at St. Paul's Cathedral in 1631, and died a few weeks later, quoting the Lord's Prayer.

"My mother did it."

ARNOLD ROTHSTEIN

True to the code of the underworld, legendary bookmaker Arnold "The Big Bankroll" Rothstein (who liked to say that the weather was the only thing he couldn't fix) refused to finger the culprits who gunned him down in a New York City hotel in 1928, at the age of 46. Rothstein is best known for allegedly fixing the 1919 Black Sox World Series, but in his lifetime he was never convicted of a single crime.

"The shadows are lengthening for me.
The twilight is here. My days of old
have vanished—tone and tints. They
have gone glimmering through the
dreams of things that were. Their
memory is one of wondrous beauty,
watered by tears and coaxed and
caressed by the smiles of yesterday.
I listen, then, but with thirsty ear, for
the witching melody of faint bugles
blowing reveille, of far drums beating
the long roll. In my dreams I hear
again the crash of guns, the rattle
of musketry, the strange, mournful
mutter of the battlefield. But in the
evening of my memory I come back
to West Point. Always there echoes
and re-echoes: duty, honor, country.
Today marks my final roll call with
you. But I want you to know that

when I cross the river, my last
conscious thoughts will be of the
corps, and the corps, and the corps.
I bid you farewell."

GENERAL
DOUGLAS MACARTHUR

———•·•·•———

Two years before he faded away in
1964, Douglas MacArthur made a final
visit to West Point, where he had been
superintendent, to deliver a farewell address.
MacArthur had a flair for the dramatic, but
he was a fearless soldier and gifted adminis-
trator. He was decorated 13 times for bravery
during World I, helped to defeat the Japanese
in World War II, and then helped to transform
Japan into a modern democracy.

"You promised me that you would help me when I could no longer carry on. It is only torture now and it has no longer any sense."

SIGMUND FREUD

A recent refugee from the Nazis and in great pain from the jaw cancer that plagued him for the last 15 years of his life, the 83-year-old founder of psychoanalysis reminded his physician of his promise to provide sedation. He received several large doses of morphine and died peacefully the next day.

"I am only asking for one thing—let me finish my work."

ISAAC BABEL

Babel, the Russian short-story master and a cosmopolitan Jew devoted to Russia, was arrested by the Soviet secret police in 1939 on false charges of espionage and terrorism. For six months, Babel lived the nightmare of absurd injustice that Kafka only imagined in his novel *The Trial*. In early 1940, Babel was forced to make a false confession and sentenced to death. These were his last recorded words before being shot to death at the age of 44.

"Fans, for the past two weeks you have been
reading about the bad break I got. Yet today
I consider myself the luckiest man on the
face of the earth. . . . Sure I'm lucky. Who
wouldn't consider it an honor to have known
Jacob Ruppert? Also, the builder of baseball's
greatest empire, Ed Barrow? To have spent
six years with that wonderful little fellow,
Miller Huggins? Then to have spent the
next nine years with that outstanding leader,
that smart student of psychology, the best
manager in baseball today, Joe McCarthy?
Sure I'm lucky. When the New York Giants,
a team you would give your right arm to
beat, and vice versa, sends you a gift—that's
something. When everybody down to the
groundskeepers and those boys in white
coats remember you with trophies—that's
something. When you have a wonderful
mother-in-law who takes sides with you in
squabbles with her own daughter—that's
something. When you have a father and a
mother who work all their lives so you can
have an education and build your body—
it's a blessing. When you have a wife who
has been a tower of strength and shown
more courage than you dreamed existed—

the finest I know. So I close in saying that
I may have had a tough break, but I have
an awful lot to live for. Thank you."

LOU GEHRIG

In 1939, before a hushed Yankee Stadium
crowd of 60,000, Lou Gehrig, who was
dying of amyotrophic lateral sclerosis (a disease that would come to bear his name),
delivered what became known as "Baseball's
Gettysburg Address." One of America's most
beloved and durable ballplayers, Gehrig was
a slugger second only to Babe Ruth. He holds
the American League record for the highest
single-season RBI total (184). And he holds
the major league record for career grand
slams, with 23.

"Let me go, the world is bobbing around me. . . . The world is a bubble. Trouble wherever you go."

SAM BASS

⋆•⫶•⋆

When frontier legend Sam Bass and his band of outlaws arrived in Round Rock, Texas, they didn't know the Texas Rangers had been tipped off about their plans to rob the local bank. On July 19, 1878, the day before the planned robbery, a shoot-out left Bass mortally wounded—and babbling badly for the next two days.

"On the contrary!"

HENRIK IBSEN

Shortly before Ibsen's death in 1906, his wife thought that she saw a marked improvement in his physical condition. "See," she exulted, "you will be quite well again," whereupon Ibsen sat up in bed and objected—with some justification, as it turned out. A Norwegian poet and playwright, Ibsen overcame a miserable youth to become the acclaimed writer of modern social dramas such as *Hedda Gabler* and *A Doll's House*.

"Death is nothing,
nor life either,
for that matter.
To die, to sleep,
to pass into
nothingness,
what does
it matter?
Everything is
an illusion."

MATA HARI

For Margareta Gertruda Zelle MacCleod, almost everything was an illusion. The Dutch wife and mother–turned–exotic dancer–turned–spy had changed her name to Mata Hari (Hindi for "Eye of the Rising Sun"), made a career in Paris out of her supposed "Indian" blood, and was finally arrested for spying for Germany in World War I. Before facing the firing squad in 1917, the 41-year-old Hari philosophized to a nun attempting to comfort her. After refusing a blindfold, Hari thanked the chief French officer, then blew her executioners a kiss.

"What is the question? If there is no question, there is no answer."

GERTRUDE STEIN

In her Paris salon, American expatriate Gertrude Stein acted as a kind of den mother, dispensing eminently quotable advice to such literary and artistic lights as Ernest Hemingway, Sherwood Anderson, Pablo Picasso, and Henri Matisse. Her final words, spoken to her longtime companion Alice B. Toklas, were vintage Stein—eccentric, existential, and enigmatic.

"They couldn't hit an elephant at this dist—."

GENERAL JOHN SEDGWICK

General John Sedgwick was a corps commander of the Army of the Potomac who enjoyed a reputation among his men as a good-humored guy and relentless optimist. At the Battle of the Wilderness, while other men were diving for cover from Confederate sharpshooters, Sedgwick scoffed at the danger, stood up, and caught a bullet in the face.

"We have been together for 40 years, and we will not separate now."

IDA STRAUS

Refusing the lifeboat offered to her, Ida Straus chose to stay aboard the sinking *Titanic* with her husband Isidor, the New York department store magnate and philanthropist. They perished together when the "unsinkable" ship slipped into the Atlantic in April of 1912.

"That's good. Go on, read some more."

WARREN G. HARDING

President Harding listened as his wife read a flattering article about him in the *Saturday Evening Post,* and lasted only long enough to express his appreciation. Most of the press he had received wasn't so complimentary; Harding led an administration roiled by corruption and cronyism. He passed away in 1923, one of four presidents to die in office of natural causes.

"The public will
never believe the
innocence of the
Clintons and their
loyal staff. I was
not meant for the
job or the spotlight
of public life in
Washington. Here
ruining people is
considered sport."

VINCENT FOSTER

Attorney Vincent Foster was a legal adviser to Bill and Hillary Clinton during their rocky first year in the White House. The Whitewater and Travel Office scandals were bearing down on him when, in 1993, police found Foster's body in a Virginia park. His death was ruled a suicide, although some right-wing groups charged that the Clintons had him killed and then covered up the murder. This note was found in his briefcase.

"[Tell them] that I loved to draw. Then go home."

EDGAR DEGAS

The French painter and sculptor didn't want a funeral oration, but if it couldn't be avoided, he told an artist friend in 1917, the eulogy should be limited to this simple sentiment. When Degas died later that year, his instructions were completely ignored.

"Drink to me!"

PABLO PICASSO

What would you expect from one of the world's most prodigious and egotistical talents but a command to be toasted on his demise in 1973 at the age of 91? The brilliant Spanish artist, unflaggingly productive and endlessly provocative, was fond of paying people by check, knowing that his creditors usually preferred keeping his valuable autograph to cashing it.

"What have I lived for?"

LORENZ HART

Although lyricist Hart successfully collaborated with composer Richard Rodgers on a number of Broadway shows, including *Pal Joey* and *On Your Toes,* he struggled with depression and alcoholism for most of his life. Hart—gay, Jewish, and very short—channeled his insecurities and unrequited feelings for Rodgers into writing. When Rodgers broke from him to join the more conventional Oscar Hammerstein, Hart went on a drinking binge, caught pneumonia in the rain, and died in 1943 at age 48.

"I've had a helluva lot of fun, and I've enjoyed every minute of it."

ERROL FLYNN

Not everyone enjoyed it as much as he, though. The handsome, bankable, swashbuckling movie star (*Captain Blood, The Adventures of Robin Hood,* and *The Sea Hawk*) was also famous for his personal hedonism, drinking, drug use, and seduction of young men and women. His 1942 trial for statutory rape—he was acquitted—spawned the expression "in like Flynn." In 1959, the dissipated actor died of a heart attack in the arms of his 15-year-old girlfriend.

"That was the best ice-cream soda I ever tasted."

LOU COSTELLO

T he portly half of the famous comedy team of Bud Abbott and Lou Costello sucked the last bit of pleasure out of his life, which ended in 1959. The two comics from New Jersey made one hit film after another in the 1940s and starred frequently on television in the 50s, but they will probably always be best known for their brilliant send-up of both baseball and language in the immortal skit "Who's on First."

"Don't cut the ham too thin."

FRED HARVEY

When restaurateur Fred Harvey died in 1901, he bade his sons one of the least sentimental good-byes in history. Harvey had revived a financially troubled railroad industry by recruiting pretty waitresses of "good character" to work in dining halls along the routes. Will Rogers once remarked that the waitresses, who came to be known as Harvey Girls, "kept the West supplied with food and wives."

"Life is still full of joy. Thumbs up for joy and adventure."

MAUDE ADAMS

So exclaimed the 81-year-old inventor and stage actress, best known for her 1905 performance as Peter Pan, as she stretched out on the sofa of her upstate New York home in 1953. No one was more disappointed than she when, a mere few hours later, she passed away.

"Tenderest love to all. Farewell, am going soon, Alice."

ALICE JAMES

A lice James was the forgotten sibling in one of America's most celebrated families. Her eldest brother, William, was perhaps the preeminent psychologist of the nineteenth century, while another, Henry, was one of its greatest novelists. Mentally fragile, she lived with her parents until their deaths, and only achieved fame posthumously with her diary. On her deathbed in 1892, Alice dictated a cable to the absent William.

"You are deep in the ages, now, deep in the ages, you whom the world could not break, nor the years tame."

SARA TEASDALE,
of Vachel Lindsay

As a young man, Vachel Lindsay toured the country on foot, paying his way with poetry. As a famous bard, he continued to travel and perform his poems. He ended his own life in 1931—poetry, health, and wealth all in decline. Fellow poet Sara Teasdale, whose epitaph is based on a line of Lindsay's poetry, also committed suicide later that same year.

"Let us cross over the river and sit under the shade of the trees."

GENERAL THOMAS "STONEWALL" JACKSON

After Robert E. Lee, no Confederate commander was more revered than Stonewall Jackson, a man as renowned for his keen battle sense as for his religious mysticism. After victories at Front Royal, Winchester, and Fredericksburg, he was accidentally shot by his own troops at Chancellorsville. Surgeons amputated his wounded left arm, but pneumonia set in. Jackson died eight days later.

"Somehow, I know you're there, Dad . . . I know you're up there saying, 'Why are you wearing that dress?'"

MELANIE GRIFFITH

———◆◆◆———

Upon arriving in Cannes to receive a special award in May 2001, the star of movies such as *Working Girl* was told that her father, businessman Peter Griffith, had died. A few days later, the actress (who was named after the character that her mother, Tippi Hedren, played in *The Birds*) paid tribute to her father's lasting influence—and sartorial judgement.

◄ 4 6 ►

"My dear, before you kiss me good-bye, fix your hair. It's a mess."

GEORGE KELLY

The Pulitzer Prize–winning playwright was famous for his parodies of American middle-class life, most notably *The Torch-Bearers, The Show-off, Craig's Wife,* and *The Deep Mrs. Sykes.* The uncle of Grace Kelly, he had high expectations for his relatives. Another, perhaps less elegant, niece attempted to kiss him farewell on his deathbed in 1974.

"I shall not trouble you much longer . . . Do you hear that? . . . That is the death rattle."

THOMAS HART BENTON

After a public brawl with Andrew Jackson in Tennessee, Thomas Hart Benton skeedaddled west to Missouri. There he became the state's first U.S. senator. In Washington, he was a tireless champion of westward expansion and a vehement opponent of slavery. His courteous last words were addressed to the black nurse who was caring for him.

"This isn't Hamlet, you know. It's not meant to go in my bloody ear!"

LAURENCE OLIVIER

So declaimed one of his generation's greatest actors on his deathbed in 1989, when Olivier's nurse spilled water on him as she tried to moisten his parched lips. Olivier's screen triumphs include his Academy Award–winning *Hamlet* in 1948, and brilliant performances in, among other films, *Rebecca* (1940), *Wuthering Heights* (1949), and *The Marathon Man* (1976).

"I wish the whole
human race had
one neck and
I had my hands
around it."

CARL PANZRAM

Mass murderer Panzram was responsible for these, perhaps the least repen-
tant words ever spoken by a condemned
man. He spat them out just before he was put
to death in Mississippi in 1930 for killing
twelve people.

"Well, folks, you'll soon see a baked Appel."

GEORGE APPEL

———

Before being put to death by electric chair in 1928 for killing a New York policeman, George Appel popped off a last line for the ages.

"Die, I should say
not, dear fellow.
No Barrymore
would allow such
a conventional
thing to happen
to him."

JOHN BARRYMORE

Though John Barrymore was wrong about not dying—he passed away soon after—he was right about the nature of his acting family. The Barrymores were drunken, headline-making eccentrics. John once threw a fish at a coughing audience member. Like his father before him, John Barrymore had four wives and countless mistresses. But when he died in 1942, he had transformed the way actors perform Shakespeare, and made the transition from the stage to silent films, and from silent films to talkies. His granddaughter Drew carries on the family acting— and headline-grabbing—tradition today.

"As to me, I leave here tomorrow for an unknown destination."

AMBROSE BIERCE

After writing this last line in a letter home, Bierce was never seen or heard from again. The American journalist disappeared in 1913, at the age of 71, presumably to roam the hills of Mexico. Rumors circulated that he was killed in Pancho Villa's revolution, while others insisted that he committed suicide in the Grand Canyon. A consummate cynic, "Bitter Bierce" wrote short stories, columns, and essays, and published the satirical *The Devil's Dictionary*. His death remains a mystery.

⊰ 5 4 ⊱

"Tell Hill he must come up . . . Strike the tent!"

ROBERT E. LEE

Abraham Lincoln offered Robert E. Lee command of the Union Army, but Lee could not imagine taking up arms against his home state, Virginia. As commander of the Confederacy's Army of Northern Virginia, he waged an ingenious yet ultimately futile campaign against the Union. Five years after surrendering to Ulysses S. Grant, Lee died, his thoughts still on the battlefield.

"Take courage, Charlotte. Take courage."

ANNE BRONTË

Anne, the second Brontë to die from tuberculosis within a year, spoke with poetic compassion from her deathbed, as she implored her older sister to find strength. The author of *The Tenant of Wildfell Hall* and *Agnes Grey* was quiet and reserved, but her novels feature unusually brave female characters.

"I'm sorry, I wish I could bring him back. I can't. Good-bye. Do it."

JOHN LAMB

J ust before being put to death with a lethal injection at the state prison near Huntsville, Texas, in 1999, Lamb apologized for killing a man who, 17 years earlier, had made a pass at him in a motel room. Earlier, he said that he would have preferred the guillotine because of his fear of needles, admitting that "I'm just afraid of the process."

"Turn up the lights. I don't want to go home in the dark."

O. HENRY

———

Sadly, the great short story writer died an alcoholic's death at 48—cirrhosis of the liver, poverty, and loneliness. Even his final words contained an allusion to the pleasures of drink. O. Henry borrowed the refrain from a song about a man who stays up all night getting drunk, but tells his wife that he won't be home till morning because "I'm afraid to come home in the dark."

"Don't pull down
the blinds. I feel fine.
I want the sunlight
to greet me."

RUDOLPH VALENTINO

A lthough desperately ill at 31 from complications from a perforated ulcer, the Roaring 20s' great cinematic Latin lover (*The Four Horsemen of the Apocalypse* and *The Sheik,* both from 1921) was not aware he was dying. His body, attired in immaculate evening dress, was viewed by thousands of stricken fans who lined up for blocks outside a New York City funeral parlor in 1926.

"More light!"

JOHANN WOLFGANG VON GOETHE

It's possible that after a lifetime in cloudy Germany, the 83-year-old poet and novelist just wanted someone to open a window and let in the sun. More likely, his last words were metaphorical. In Goethe's lyrical drama, *Faust,* the word "light" comes up again and again as a spiritual metaphor. Goethe's light went out in 1831, when he died in his favorite armchair.

"Water!"

ULYSSES S. GRANT

Having braved throat cancer to finish one of the greatest and most plain-spoken autobiographies ever written, the man who led the Union to victory in the American Civil War 20 years before expired in 1885 after making this last request. He had survived scandal during his two terms as president before Mark Twain convinced him to put everything down in what became a bestselling book.

"To die is one of two things, for either the dead may be annihilated and have no sensation of anything whatever, or, as it is said, there are a certain change and passage of the soul from one place to another. And if it is a privation of all sensation—as it were, a sleep, in which the sleeper has no dream—death would be a wonderful gain . . . if, therefore, death is a thing of this kind I say it is a gain: for thus all futurity appears to be nothing more than one night. But if so, the other hand, death is a removal from one plane to another, and what is said is true, that all the dead are there, and what greater blessing can there be than this, my judges? But this is clear to me, that now to die and be freed of my cares is better for me . . . but it is now time to depart, for me to die, for you to live. But which of us is going to a better state is unknown to everyone but God."

SOCRATES

We remember the Greek philosopher Socrates as a martyr for intellectual inquiry. In his own day, he was regarded as a nuisance who stopped busy people on the street to ask annoying questions about the meaning of life. Before his execution, Socrates remembered that he "owed a cock to Asclepius"; he asked his friend Crito to stand in for him.

"Bless you, Sister, may all your sons be bishops."

BRENDAN BEHAN

———————

S o, with characteristic irony, spoke the Irish playwright and author to a hospital nun moments before he died of alcohol- and diabetes-related complications in 1964. Behan channeled the pain of his years as a political prisoner (at age 16, he was caught carrying explosives for the IRA) into writing, and created profound and irreverent works like *Borstal Boy, The Quare Fellow,* and *The Hostage.*

"I knew it. I knew it.
Born in a hotel room—
and God damn it—
died in a hotel room."

EUGENE O'NEILL

O'Neill, winner of four Pulitzer Prizes and the 1936 Nobel Prize for Literature, spent the first several years of his life in hotels, following his father on tour. His most successful plays were about dysfunctional family life, an area with which he was very familiar. His mother, a morphine addict, attempted suicide, and his eldest son was successful at it. O'Neill, never satisfied with his life, was not satisfied with his death either.

"The machinery is worn out."

WOODROW WILSON

Horrified by the devastation of World War I, President Woodrow Wilson threw his support behind the League of Nations, a proto-United Nations. In a nationwide whistle-stop campaign, he tried to win the support of the American people. Exhausted by his travels and heartbroken by the Senate's rejection of the League, Wilson suffered a stroke from which he never truly recovered. He died in 1924, three years after leaving office.

"Tell my former friends in New York that the old man looks as if he might live ten years longer."

CHARLES BEARD

Soon after making this prediction in 1948, historian Charles Beard proved himself entirely wrong by dying at the age of 74. The progressive Beard, a Quaker, was active in opposing U.S. entry into World War I. Later, he was named in the Red Scare of 1919–20, after which he was unable to land an academic appointment, forcing him to live off his writings and his Connecticut dairy farm.

"Walter, who knows what is the scheme of things. My suffering has all been for the purpose of making you a man."

MOSES ANNENBERG

A month after his 1942 release from prison, where he served two years for income tax evasion, the powerful immigrant-turned–publishing tycoon (the *Morning Telegraph,* the *Daily Racing Form,* and the *Philadelphia Inquirer*) expired with these poignant and paternal words. Annenberg had pleaded guilty, in exchange for which the prosecution dropped additional charges against his son and protégé, Walter. Walter vindicated his father's suffering by turning the family business into a respectable enterprise, and by eventually giving away billions of dollars to education and the arts.

"I shall be dead in a
quarter of an hour.
To die by the hand of
one's own people is
hard. But the house is
surrounded, and Hitler
is charging me with
high treason. In view of
my services in Africa, I
am to have the chance
of dying by poison . . .
if I accept, none of the
usual steps will be
taken against my

family, that is, against
you . . . they will also
leave my staff alone."

ERWIN ROMMEL

The German field marshal impressed
Hitler enough to be made a general in
1939, two years before he earned the name
"The Desert Fox" for his success with
Hitler's Afrika Corps in Libya. However, by
1944, Rommel had lost respect for his leader
and agreed to assist in a failed assassination
attempt. He spoke these last words to his son
Manfred shortly before he took the poison
ordered by the monster he had once served
so well.

"Throw a quilt over her."

FREDERICK THE GREAT

E mperor Frederick the Great of Prussia was a splendid ruler. During his long reign in the late 18th century, he abolished religious persecution, established a free press, and protected private property. Nonetheless, he believed his subjects were ignorant cattle and reserved his affection for his army and his pet dogs. From his deathbed, he saw his favorite greyhound shivering, and issued this order to his valet.

"You get on with your life. I've got to go."

SEATTLE SLEW

With a right front foot that curved out-ward, the young Seattle Slew didn't look promising. Yet he ended his racing career having won 14 out of 17 races and the 1977 Triple Crown. When he died, Slew's devoted owner, Mickey Taylor, was at his side. "Chet, my black Labrador, licked Slew's face and then Slew licked Chet's face," said Taylor. "Then Slew looked up at me and said, 'You get on with your life. I've got to go.'"

"Curtain! Fast music! Light! Ready for the last finale! Great! The show looks good, the show looks good!"

FLORENZ ZIEGFELD

Ziegfeld, whose most famous extravaganzas were the *Ziegfeld Follies* and *Showboat,* was a born promoter. He got his start selling his friends tickets to see "invisible fish"—otherwise known as a bowl of water. His last shows bombed, hampered by Ziegfeld's gambling losses and the Great Depression. As he died, he hallucinated one last show—a surefire hit.

"Get my swan costume ready."

ANNA PAVLOVA

The world-famous Russian ballerina rejected an operation for pleurisy that could have saved her life but would have damaged her ribs, leaving her unable to perform. Her dying words, a reference to her acclaimed performances in *Swan Lake,* seemed to confirm to what extent ballet had been her life.

"That was a great game of golf, fellers."

BING CROSBY

R emembered today as a major movie star and the crooner who gave us the definitive performance of "White Christmas," Bing Crosby was also an ardent and accomplished golfer. He had just finished a round in which he and his partner trounced two golf pros when he suffered a fatal heart attack, 20 yards from the clubhouse.

"Then let's forget about it, and play high five."

BUFFALO BILL CODY

In 1917, the legendary cowboy, showman, and buffalo hunter asked his doctor how much time he had left. The doctor gave him a sobering estimate: "Your life is like an hour glass. The sand is slipping away gradually. Slowly, but surely, the sand will be gone. The end is not far away." Cody was not perturbed.

"I am reconciled to my
death, but I detest the
mode . . . it will be but
a momentary pang.
I pray you bear witness
that I met my fate
like a brave man."

JOHN ANDRÉ

The 29-year-old British major penned
this letter to General Henry Clinton, asking to die a soldier's death before a firing
squad rather than be hanged as a spy for con-
spiring with Benedict Arnold for the handover
of West Point. André's request went unheeded.

"Lift me up, for I am dying. I shall die easy. Don't be frightened. Thank God it has come."

JOHN KEATS

Lyrical to the last, the precocious British poet, the son of a livery stable keeper, succumbed at 26 to tuberculosis, with his friend Joseph Severn at his side. Keats's writing career lasted little more than five years, ending with his death in 1821, but his work has achieved immortality.

"Why not? After all, it belongs to Him."

CHARLIE CHAPLIN

So said Chaplin on his deathbed in 1977 to an attending priest who prayed, "May the Lord have mercy on your soul." World-famous for his cinematic silence, offscreen the British-born comedian was both a lot of talk and action. In 1919, he helped found his own studio, United Artists, to control his own Hollywood fate. He had less control elsewhere; disgusted in the 1950s by right-wing attempts to paint him as a communist, he eventually settled in Switzerland.

"Why should I talk to you? I've just been talking to your boss."

WILSON MIZNER

On his deathbed in 1933, con artist, dramatist, and wit Wilson Mizner briefly regained consciousness to find a priest there. From the late 1800s through the 1930s, Wilson and his brother Addison traveled from Florida to Alaska bilking people out of their money, often with a sense of humor. He once entered a candy store with a gun and a black mask, shouting, "Your chocolates or your life!"

"Good, a woman who can fart is not dead."

COMTESSE DE VERCELLIS

I n 1728, after breaking wind, the aristocratic comtesse uttered these words to an embarrassed visitor. Moments later, she was dead—though not from the flatulence. The French philosopher Jean Jacques Rouseau, one of her lackeys, immortalized her final words in his autobiographical work, *Confessions*.

"Mind your own business."

WYNDHAM LEWIS

A sked about the functioning of his bowels shortly before his death, the 73-year-old Lewis answered sharply. In 1914, Lewis, a Canadian/British painter and author, founded Vorticism, an artistic movement that emphasized angle and line, violence and machinery. Like his friend Ezra Pound, Lewis was a fascist, though his politics evolved through the years. In his personal life, he was lonely and secretive, as his last words suggest.

"What is the news? Are there any messages?"

CLARENCE W. BARRON

⬩━━━⬩

S ome businessmen live at the office, but few die there. Barron, president of Dow Jones and Company and publisher of *The Wall Street Journal,* was one of them. In 1928, he asked his secretary a couple of routine questions, and died moments later.

"How are the Mets doing today?"

MOE BERG

The former major league catcher and coach, a reputed spy for the U.S. government, was baseball's greatest international man of mystery and an enigma even to those closest to him. The erudite ballplayer could speak half a dozen languages, but couldn't, it was said, hit in any of them. Although he played mostly for American League teams in the 1920s and 30s, he was thinking of the National League's New York Mets, his favorite club, when he lay dying in 1972 at the age of 69.

"It's nearly over. I know it and we must face it. Go out and have a good cry. Don't make it a long one. This is something we can't help."

CHRISTY MATHEWSON

As he lay dying of tuberculosis in 1925, Mathewson tried to console his wife. Unlike many teammates, he avoided hard drink and fast women. Fastballs were another matter. In his 17-year career, spent mostly with the New York Giants, Mathewson won 373 games, including 80 shutouts.

"This is a mortal wound. Take care of that pistol. It is undischarged and still cocked. It might go off and do harm. I did not intend to fire at him."

ALEXANDER HAMILTON

Founding Father Hamilton's life ebbed away on a New Jersey field in 1804 after he lost a duel with political nemesis Aaron Burr. Burr challenged Hamilton to the duel after the latter's denunciation of him helped ruin his bid for the New York governorship.

"You're up on your beautiful Appaloosa stallion. It's a fine spring day. We're riding through the woods. The bluebells are all out, and the sky is a clear blue."

PAUL McCARTNEY
on his wife Linda, after her death

Doing things together had been a hallmark of Paul and Linda McCartney's long and happy marriage. The former Beatle and his wife had gone riding just two days before her death from breast cancer in 1998. Linda's creativity and environmental activism had a huge influence on Sir Paul; when asked what tribute Linda would like best, Paul replied: "Go veggie."

"I've seen the promised land. And I may not get there with you. But I want you to know tonight that we, as a people, will get to the promised land . . . I'm happy tonight. I'm not worried about anything.

Mine eyes have seen the glory of the coming of the Lord."

MARTIN LUTHER KING, JR.

Martin Luther King, Jr., the black civil rights leader, Baptist preacher, and Nobel Peace Prize winner, was killed by an assassin's bullet in April 1968. The day before he died, King delivered a last, prophetic speech before a group of sanitation workers in Memphis.

"Kiss me, Hardy."

ADMIRAL HORATIO NELSON

Admiral Horatio Nelson's brilliant command of the British Navy at Trafalgar frustrated Napoléon's scheme to invade England. But during the battle, Nelson was mortally wounded by a French sniper's bullet. All his life he had been aloof and ambitious; now, as he lay dying in the arms of one of his officers, Nelson craved a little human affection.

"I am in a duel to death with this wallpaper. One of us has to go."

OSCAR WILDE

W itty till the end, the notorious aesthete and Beethoven of the bon mot is said to have fired off this one a month before he expired in 1900. (Other sources claim his *last* words were, "Alas, I'm dying beyond my means," said while he sipped champagne.) After marrying and fathering two sons, the acerbic Irish playwright and novelist was sent to prison for "homosexual offenses," was released in 1897, and spent his final years in France.

"Hurry back."

HUMPHREY BOGART

❦

So Bogart told his actress-wife, Lauren Bacall, as she left for the grocery store. He was dead by the time she returned. The duo starred opposite each other in 1940s film noirs like *To Have and Have Not* and *The Big Sleep,* and enjoyed sultry chemistry on and off the screen. The marriage lasted until Bogart's death from throat cancer in 1957.

"Oh, God, here I go!"

MAX ADELBERT BAER

Max Adelbert Baer was the world boxing heavyweight champion from 1934 to 1935. He racked up 72 wins, 12 losses, and one no-decision. But here's the statistic that really packs a punch: of his 72 wins, 53 were knockouts, including one man that he killed. The champ uttered these parting words as he was KO'ed by a massive heart attack in 1959 at the age of 50.

"I don't know which is more difficult in a Christian life—to live well or to die well."

DANIEL DEFOE

Dying—at least in the case of the 70-year-old Defoe, who died alone and deeply indebted in a London boarding house in 1731. A devout Presbyterian, Defoe wrote *Robinson Crusoe,* about a shipwrecked man who talks to God and converts a cannibal to Christianity. The author was no stranger to dying declarations— to make some extra money, he had once forged the "last words" of condemned criminals, and sold them to a greedy public.

"It is. But it's not as hard as farce."

EDMUND GWENN

It was actor Jack Lemmon who asked Gwenn near the end if dying was difficult. An English stage actor originally discovered by George Bernard Shaw, Gwenn did not became a Hollywood star until middle age, and continued acting into his eighties. Twice nominated for an Academy Award, he won Best Supporting Actor honors for his role as Santa Claus in *Miracle on 34th Street*.

"I want to go . . . God take me!"

DWIGHT EISENHOWER

I n March, 1969, after surviving seven heart attacks and recurring bouts of congestive heart failure, Dwight D. Eisenhower was ready to go. The life he left behind was remarkable: graduate of West Point; commander of the Allied Forces landing in France on D-Day, 1944; commanding general of the victorious Allies in Europe; president of Columbia University; and president of the United States—twice.

"Glory, Hallelujah. I'm going to the Lordy. I come, ready, go!"

CHARLES JULIUS GUITEAU

In 1881, a "divine revelation" inspired this failed lawyer and religious zealot to assassinate President James Garfield in order to unite the Republican party. Guiteau's trial was one of the first in which lawyers employed insanity as a defense—their client believed he was an agent of God—but they could not save him. His last words did little to confirm his sanity.

"Oh God, have pity on my soul. Oh God, have pity on my soul."

ANNE BOLEYN

———•═•═•———

It's not surprising that Anne Boleyn, the second of Henry VIII's six wives and the mother of Elizabeth I, asked for God's pity at the end. Henry broke from the pope and divorced his first wife to marry Boleyn, only to have her beheaded in 1536 after she failed to produce a male heir. The day before the execution, she comforted herself by musing that "the executioner is, I believe, very expert, and my neck is very slender."

"All my possessions for a moment of time."

ELIZABETH I,
QUEEN OF ENGLAND

"The Virgin Queen" was a great flirt, but dead serious about power. Under her reign (1558–1603), England became a world power—and literature, education, fashion, and glamour all flourished. The clothes of the Elizabethan era were fabulous, none more so than those of the queen, whose gowns dripped with jewels and gems. Although she was twice accused of treason, she remains one of England's best-loved rulers.

"I'm tired of fighting. I guess this thing is going to get me."

HARRY HOUDINI

With these words, magician and escape artist extraordinaire Harry Houdini performed his final disappearing act. The man who astonished millions with his ability to extricate himself from ropes, chains, manacles, strait jackets, sealed trunks, and even a water-torture cell, fell victim on Halloween in 1926 to a simple case of appendicitis (and not, as many claim, to a college student's punch in the stomach).

"Sister, you're trying to keep me alive as an old curiosity. But I'm done, I'm finished, I'm going to die."

GEORGE BERNARD SHAW

The Irish playwright was a brilliant curiosity—a socialist vegetarian feminist who believed himself to be Shakespeare reincarnated. His most celebrated play, *Pygmalion,* was made into the musical *My Fair Lady*, earning him the double distinction of an Academy Award and a Nobel Prize. In 1950, at 94, he fell off a ladder and died with his sister at his side.

"She was awful— and she was worth it."

A EULOGIST SPEAKING AT THE FUNERAL OF LILLIAN HELLMAN

—•••—

This comment at the 1984 funeral of the acerbic, brilliant, and mean-spirited playwright *(The Children's Hour, The Little Foxes)* and memoirist *(An Unfinished Woman, Pentimento)* was on target. Hellman was a woman even her friends loved to loathe.

"She still fascinates me . . ."

RICHARD BURTON

The hard-living and hard-guzzling Welsh actor met Elizabeth Taylor on the set of *Cleopatra* in 1962 and they soon began one of the great public love stories of the century. Of all his many conquests and wives (he married Taylor twice, the second union ending in 1976), she was the one on his mind, he confided to friend and fellow actor John Hurt, shortly before he died in 1984 at the age of 59.

"Maria, don't let me die!"

D. H. LAWRENCE

As he lost his battle with tuberculosis in 1930 at the age of 44, British novelist Lawrence cried out deliriously, "Look at him, there in the bed!" Moments later, the brilliant and troubled writer called out for his friend, Maria Christina Chambers. Lawrence, perhaps most famous for the sexually explicit *Lady Chatterley's Lover,* had wasted away to a mere eighty-five pounds at the end.

"God, don't let me die. I have so much to do."

HUEY LONG

The flamboyant, populist "Kingfish" of Louisiana politics won voters' hearts through demagoguery, and got roads and bridges built and the state university expanded by his masterful manipulation of Democratic party machine politics. He inspired Robert Penn Warren's classic novel *All The King's Men*. His ambitions—among them, to challenge FDR for the presidency—were on his mind as he lay dying from an assassin's bullet in 1935.

"See that Yul gets star billing. He has earned it."

GERTRUDE LAWRENCE

A grand dame of the English and American stage, Gertrude Lawrence was renowned for her performance opposite Noël Coward in Coward's *Private Lives*. Her final role was playing Anna in the Rodgers and Hammerstein musical *The King and I*. As she was dying of liver cancer, she put in a good word for her co-star, Yul Brynner, who was playing the king.

"What an artist the world is losing in me."

NERO

When Nero, the vain and brutal Roman emperor, built a new palace on top of the ruins of the Great Fire of 64, people blamed him for setting the fire. The expression "Nero fiddled as Rome burned" arose from these suspicions, as well as from his habit of forcing everyone to listen to him play his instrument. When the public and his generals finally turned on him in A.D. 68, the 31-year-old Nero committed suicide.

"There's fun in the air."

MAURICE CHEVALIER

J ust before slipping into a coma at the age of 84, the French charmer and actor whispered these words to Father Alain Carré. Ironically, the phrase comes from a famous song by Charles Trenet, with whom Chevalier had been feuding for years.

"You know, my fun days are over."

JAMES DEAN

The young actor's remark to a friend was eerily prophetic. Only days later, he died while speeding in his silver Porsche Spyder near Paso Robles, California, just after finishing the movie *Giant*. Although his film career—which also included *Rebel Without A Cause* and *East of Eden* (the only one of his major movies that had been released when he died)—was cut short at the age of 24, the actor has lived on as a legend and as the American archetype of the sensitive rebel.

"You know, I actually believe that the medical profession can produce scientific men who are sufficiently sincere in thinking that they can extend human flesh forever. I told my doctor when he came at 6:30 this morning to see about my coming down here. I said, 'Do you think that you have a patient, or will ever have a patient, that you can keep alive forever?' I think he sometimes thinks that . . . I don't believe that

I'm going to be able to speak any longer . . ."

BRANCH RICKEY

———✦———

Baseball impresario Branch Rickey was famous for two things: talking incessantly, and breaking baseball's color barrier in 1947 by signing Jackie Robinson to the Brooklyn Dodgers. Rickey was in the middle of a long-winded acceptance speech at Missouri's Sports Hall of Fame when he collapsed in mid-sentence. He never regained consciousness.

"Oh, I am not going to die, am I? He will not separate us, we have been so happy."

CHARLOTTE BRONTË

———•·•·•———

After managing to avoid contracting tuberculosis—the disease that killed her four sisters and mother—Brontë succumbed to pernicious morning sickness while pregnant in 1855, after only one year of marriage. Standing at just 4' 9", Brontë far surpassed her stature in talent, leaving a brilliant legacy in fiction, perhaps most notably with *Jane Eyre*.

"Goodnight, my darlings, I'll see you tomorrow."

NOËL COWARD

T he playwright and favorite of London's theater scene was determined to end his life with the perfect witticism, but a heart attack foiled his plans. On March 25, 1973, Coward bid a prosaic goodnight to his friend Cole Presley and long-time lover Graham Payne, and died the next morning on his estate in Jamaica.

"Dear world,
I'm leaving you
because I'm bored.
I am leaving you
with your worries.
Good luck."

GEORGE SANDERS

S anders kissed the world good-bye with these words in his handwritten suicide note. The British actor, who invariably played suave but jaded characters on the screen, wore out in 1972 at the age of 66. He checked into a hotel in Barcelona and checked out with an overdose of sleeping pills.

"It wasn't worth it."

LOUIS B. MAYER

The last scene of legendary MGM movie mogul Louis B. Mayer's life was played out in a hospital room at Cedars of Lebanon Hospital in Los Angeles in 1957. If the 72-year-old Mayer's depressing line of dialogue had been written for an MGM death scene, it no doubt would have ended up on the cutting-room floor.

"Sing to me if you have the heart."

HORACE MANN

⊶•◦•⊷

Horace Mann wanted every American child to have what he never had himself—a solid education. He set up the first public grammar school in Lexington, Massachusetts, and by the time he died in 1859, public schools were common throughout the United States. But at the end, what he wanted most was to hear his wife sing.

"I shall hear in heaven!"

LUDWIG VAN BEETHOVEN

D eafness afflicted the great German composer from the time he was 31 years old. When he lay dying of pneumonia in 1827 at the age of 57, he is said to have raged at God during a violent thunderstorm. (Other sources claim his last words were: "Friends, applaud. The comedy is over.")

"Goodbye, I'll see you in heaven."

JOHN D. ROCKEFELLER, SR.

"**Y**ou will if you get in," Henry Ford replied. As a lifelong churchgoer, John D. Rockefeller had always believed that when his end came, the angels would welcome him with open arms. But people who knew Rockefeller—such as fellow tycoon Henry Ford—had their doubts. Would Heaven really overlook the old robber baron's greed and the cold-hearted business practices he used to steamroll his competition?

"Hang on to
the Matchless Mine.
Silver is coming back.
It will make you
rich again."

HORACE TABOR

———•◦•———

Prospector Horace Tabor hit pay dirt in the silver mines of Colorado. But when his mines went bust, Tabor had no reserves to keep him and his wife, Baby Doe, living the high life. Still, he clung to the forlorn hope that there was more silver to be found in his panned-out Matchless Mine. He was dead wrong.

"I am dying. I haven't drunk champagne for a long time."

ANTON CHEKHOV

Chekhov, author of *The Three Sisters, The Seagull,* and *Uncle Vanya,* was a genius at fusing the comic and the tragic in Russian daily life. His plays have survived as masterpieces of modern theater, his short stories as timeless literary gems. While suffering the final throes of tuberculosis in 1904, his last request was both simple and poignant.

"I have just had
18 whiskeys in a row.
I do believe that
is a record."

DYLAN THOMAS

⸻ •◦• ⸻

This boast, by the ebullient and bibulous 20th-century Welsh poet, was made in 1953 to staff members at Bellevue Hospital, where Thomas had been taken during one of his several successful reading tours of the United States. It would be his last. Shortly after announcing his record-breaking achievement, the poet died at the age of 39.

"Cool it, brothers."

MALCOLM X

B orn Malcolm Little, charismatic black activist Malcolm X broke with Nation of Islam founder Elijah Muhammad in 1964 and worked to cooperate with more moderate groups. While asking black Muslim factions to resolve their differences in a 1965 speech, he was assassinated by rivals as he stood at the podium in Harlem's Audubon Ballroom.

"I don't mind if my life goes in the service of the nation. If I die today, every drop of my blood will invigorate the nation."

INDIRA GANDHI

Indian prime minister Gandhi was assassinated the next day by her bodyguards. She had used patriotism to justify her repressive policies, once declaring a state of "emergency" in order to imprison her enemies and suspend constitutional rights.

"A dying man can do nothing easy."

BEN FRANKLIN

Ben Franklin—Founding Father, inventor, polymath, diplomat—remains one of America's most quoted public figures. In 1732, Franklin published *Poor Richard's Almanac,* a collection of useful facts and proverbs that included "Early to bed, and early to rise, makes a man healthy, wealthy and wise"—advice he rarely followed. In 1790, when Franklin's daughter suggested that her dying father shift positions so that he might "breathe easier," the 84-year-old produced one last maxim.

"We don't know what he did, but he sure looked tired."

SENATOR PAUL WELLSTONE

In the Senate gym, former college wrestler Paul Wellstone held the senatorial record for push-ups and chin-ups. But on the Senate floor, this unabashed Minnesota liberal lost most ideological scrimmages. Shortly before he died in a plane crash in 2002, his friend, former Senator Bob Kerrey, asked Wellstone what he would like carved on his headstone. This was his answer.

"Just a lot of damnfoolery!"

OLIVER WENDELL HOLMES

Supreme Court Justice Oliver Wendell Holmes, the "Great Dissenter," remained crusty until the end. In cases in 1919 and 1925, his dissent laid the groundwork for the protection of speech that did not present a "clear and present danger." At age 94, while gazing at an oxygen tent being rigged around him, he snorted his last opinion.

"I'm glad to meet an honest judge."

FIORELLO H. LaGUARDIA

❧

Fiorello LaGuardia summed up his political philosophy in this tribute to Judge Learned Hand, one of the last people to see the New York City mayor before he died of pancreatic cancer in 1947. LaGuardia was a lifelong opponent of machine politics and judges on the take, and a tireless champion of government that fed and housed the poor, fought crime, and built more schools and parks.

"Ah, Rouen, I have great fear you will suffer by my death! . . . Jesus, Jesus . . ."

JOAN OF ARC

A t the insistence of the "voices" of saints, this peasant girl disguised herself as a man and led 3,000 French troops to victory over the English at Orleans in 1429. In 1431, she was condemned by an English-dominated church court for claiming to receive direct inspiration from God. Joan, who would have to wait until 1920 to officially become a saint in the Vatican's eyes, was burned at the stake in Rouen, calling out Jesus' name as the flames engulfed her.

"I want nothing but death."

JANE AUSTEN

A fter her death in 1817, Jane Austen's brother wrote that "on all subjects [Jane] had ideas as clear as her expressions were well chosen." Novelist Austen—whose works include *Pride and Prejudice, Emma,* and *Northanger Abbey*—succumbed to Addison's disease at 42. In her final hours, when her sister asked her if she wanted anything, Austen suggested, with both sense and sensibility, that at the very end there is little use in wanting anything but death.

"I am about to die
and am not afraid
to die. I thank you
for your attention
and I pray you
to take no more
trouble for me.
Let me go quietly,
I cannot last long."

GEORGE WASHINGTON

Washington, our country's first president, was also the country's first hero. Had he chosen to do so, George Washington could have been America's president in perpetuity. Instead, he went home to Virginia after serving two terms. When he died in 1799, his friend Henry Lee eulogized him with words that have since been memorized by many generations of Americans: "He was the first in war, first in peace, and first in the hearts of his countrymen."

"Oh, Lord God Almighty, as thou wilt!"

JAMES BUCHANAN

Buchanan surrendered his power—characteristically—in a dying declaration to God. As president, he failed to use federal authority to stop the growing North–South tensions that helped bring on the Civil War. The day before he died, Buchanan insisted that he meant well, and that history would vindicate him. It hasn't; he is usually rated one of American's worst presidents.

"Sleep well, my sweetheart. Please don't worry too much."

ROB HALL

A world-class climber and guide to high-altitude destinations, Rob Hall met his wife, Jan Arnold, on the slopes of Mount Everest. In 1996, Hall was leading eight climbers down from the world's highest mountain when a violent storm hit unexpectedly. Trapped without shelter, certain that he was about to die, Hall made this farewell call to his wife.

"Hi, Jules. It's Brian. I'm on a plane and we've been hijacked, and it doesn't look good. Hopefully, I'll talk to you again, but if not, please have fun and live your life the best you can. Know that I love you, and no

matter what I'll
see you again
someday."

BRIAN SWEENEY

A t 8:58 A.M. on September 11, 2001, Brian Sweeney, a businessman who had once flown F-14s for the Navy, was on his cell phone trying to reach his wife, Julie. She wasn't home, so he said good-bye into the answering machine. Moments later, Sweeney's plane, United Flight 175 from Boston to Los Angeles, crashed into New York's World Trade Center.

"I paint as a means to make life bearable. Don't weep. What I have done is best for all of us. No use, I shall never be rid of this depression."

VINCENT VAN GOGH

The relationship between art and unhappiness has perhaps never been so poignantly expressed. Dutch painter Vincent Van Gogh left these words behind before killing himself in 1890 with a gunshot to his chest at the age of 37. In a mad flurry of activity in Arles, France, during the last two years of his life, Van Gogh cut off his left earlobe, but painted some of his most ecstatic works.

"Dearest,

I feel certain that I am going mad again.
I feel we can't go through another of those
terrible times. And I shan't recover this
time. I begin to hear voices, and can't
concentrate. So I am doing what seems
the best thing to do. You have given me
the greatest possible happiness. You have
been in every way all that anyone could be.
I don't think two people could have been
happier till this terrible disease came.
I can't fight it any longer. I know that I
am spoiling your life, that without me
you could work. And you will now I know.
You see I can't even write this properly.
I can't read. What I want to say is that
I owe all the happiness of life to you.
You have been entirely patient with me
and incredibly good. I want to say that—
everybody knows it. If anybody could
have saved me it would have been you.

Everything has gone from me but the certainty of your goodness. I can't go on spoiling your life any longer. I don't think two people could have been happier than we have been. V."

VIRGINIA WOOLF

After surviving an earlier suicide attempt, Woolf went on to become one of the most important and prolific writers in modern England, with works such as *The Waves, To the Lighthouse,* and the feminist essay *A Room of One's Own.* In spite of her success, mental illness continued to plague her, and on March 28, 1941, she left a note for her husband, Leonard, filled her pockets with rocks, and drowned herself in England's River Ouse.

"Now listen, Phil, fun is fun.
Aha . . . please! Papa!
What happened to the
sixteen? . . . Oh, oh, dog
biscuit, and when he is
happy he doesn't get snappy.
. . . There are only ten of
us and there are ten million
fighting somewhere in
front of you, so get your
onions up and we will throw
up a truce flag. He eats like
a little sausage baloney
maker. . . . Oh, sir, and get
the doll a roofing. Please.

You can play jacks, and
girls do that with a soft
ball and do tricks with it.
Please—I may take all
events into consideration. . . .
The sidewalks were in
trouble and the bears were
in trouble and I broke it
up. My gilt-edges stuff
and those dirty rats have
tuned in. Please, Mother,
you pick me up now.
A boy has never wept,
nor dashed a thousand
kiln. Please crackdown

on the Chinaman's friends
and Hitler's commander.
Mother is the best bet
and don't let Satan draw
you too fast. I am half-crazy.
They won't let me get up.
They dyed my shoes.
Give me something.
I am so sick. Give me
some water, the only
thing I want."

DUTCH SCHULTZ

And the award for Most Annoying Last Words goes to infamous mobster Arthur Flegenheimer (alias Dutch Schultz), who rambled feverishly for many pages (these are just excerpts; a police stenographer took it all down) as he lay dying in Newark City Hospital after being ambushed by assassins at a Newark, New Jersey, restaurant in 1935. To this day, nobody can figure out what the hell he was talking about.

"Go on, get out. Last words are for fools who haven't said enough!"

KARL MARX

———•◦•———

German social philosopher Karl Marx sought to change the world with *Das Kapital* and the Communist Manifesto. The father of communism passed away in 1883 after delivering these two sentences, which, alas, have lived on as exactly what he feared: last words.

"In the name of God, please let me die in peace!"

VOLTAIRE

On his deathbed in 1778, the French Enlightenment philosopher, writer, and author Francois Marie Arouet (pen name "Voltaire") was asked if he would finally recognize the divinity of Jesus Christ. Voltaire, who spent his life fighting ignorance and violence, and who was well known to embrace Deism rather than Christianity, was having none of it.

"You know how bad my voice
sounds. Well, it feels just as
bad. You know, this baseball
game of ours comes up from
the youth. That means the
boys. . . . The only real game
in the world, I think, is
baseball . . . you've got to start
way down at the bottom, when
you're six or seven years old . .
. you've got to let it grow up
with you, and if you're
successful and try hard
enough, you're bound to come
out on top, just like these boys
have come to the top now.
There's been so many lovely

things said about me. I'm glad I had the opportunity to thank everyone."

GEORGE HERMAN
"BABE" RUTH

At a Baltimore orphanage/reform school, Brother Matthias taught an unruly seven-year-old named Babe Ruth how to play baseball. What the future Hall-of-Famer and "Sultan of Swat" learned as a boy eventually paid off—for him, the New York Yankees, and the game of baseball. On April 27, 1947, dying of cancer, Ruth bid farewell to fans at a Yankee Stadium ceremony.

"I had it all, I did it all, I loved it all."

SID LUCKMAN

❦

That's what Luckman wanted—and got— carved on his headstone. The legendary Chicago Bears quarterback revolutionized offense in the 1940s with the T-formation, was named NFL Most Valuable Player three times, and All-Pro seven times. He is the Bears' all-time leader in career touchdowns thrown (137) and passing yards (14,686). In the 1940 title game, he led Chicago to a 73–0 victory over Washington —still the most lopsided game in NFL history.

"I always talk better lying down."

PRESIDENT
JAMES MADISON

Standing up, Madison was only 5'4", making him the tiniest chief executive in history. He had helped shape his young country by serving in the Continental Congress, framing the Bill of Rights, and earning the moniker "Father of the Constitution"—all before he was elected as the fourth U.S. president. His vivacious wife, Dolley, also played her part: She saved an important portrait of George Washington from the burning capital during the War of 1812.

"I do not have to forgive my enemies. I have had them all shot."

RAMÓN MARIA NARVAEZ

So replied the dying Spanish general to a priest's inquiry. Narvaez had used violence and suppression to consolidate power for the Conservative party and Queen Isabel II, and they had rewarded him with several high government positions, including that of prime minister. Narvaez died in office in Madrid in 1868.

"From one Christian to another, I love you."

CONNIE RAY EVANS

I n 1987, the state of Mississippi chose to deal with a tide of anti-crime fervor by randomly choosing death-row inmates to be executed. Evans, who had killed a convenience store clerk, was the second one selected to go to Parchman Penitentiary's new gas chamber. Evans's last words perhaps lend credence to a description of him as "a relatively mild soul"—for a murderer, that is.

"Take me home. I was born in the South and I wish to die and be buried in the South."

BOOKER T. WASHINGTON

Born in slavery, Booker T. Washington, founder of the Tuskegee Institute, devoted his life to helping the newly freed slaves of the South achieve economic independence. Since most Southerners hated Washington and his ideas, he turned to white Northerners for financial support. But, when all was said and done, he wished to return to the region that had never wanted him.

"I do not regret this journey, which has shown that Englishmen can endure hardship . . . and meet death with as great a fortitude as ever in the past."

ROBERT FALCON SCOTT

The 1912 race to the South Pole featured Roald Amundsen, a man of science, and Robert Falcon Scott, a romantic who put his faith in British pluck and luck. Science won. Even in his final hours, Scott couldn't see he would have lived with proper equipment.

"Here lies Robert Maxwell. He lies everywhere else."

PRIVATE EYE MAGAZINE

Not long after media magnate Robert Maxwell was reported missing from his private yacht in November 1991, his body was recovered off the Canary Islands. Glowing eulogies quickly turned to condemnations as the scope of Maxwell's dishonesty was uncovered. *Private Eye,* one of Britain's premier satirical magazines, offered this biting epitaph.

"That's a very good one. Tomorrow I will be telling it on the Golden Floor."

A.E. HOUSMAN

———

This was Housman's response on his deathbed to being told an off-color joke by his doctor. Though he failed his final exams at Oxford in 1881, Housman went on to become an illustrious poet and scholar. "Golden" was one of his favorite words, and his dying reference to "the Golden Floor" was a fitting ending to his love affair with the adjective.

"After I saw the country of
my own language fall, and
my spiritual land, Europe,
destroying itself, and, as I
reach the age of sixty, it
would require enormous
strength to reconstruct
my life, and my energy
is exhausted by long
years of peregrination
as one without a country.
Therefore, I believe it is
time to end a life which was
dedicated only to spiritual
work, considering human

liberty and my own as the greatest wealth in the world. I leave an affectionate good-bye to all my friends."

STEFAN ZWEIG

A renowned poet, dramatist, and novelist, and son of a well-to-do Viennese Jewish family, Stefan Zweig was psychologically unprepared for the rise of Nazism in his native Austria. He went into exile, first in England, then in Brazil. There, in 1942, fearful that Hitler would win the war, Zweig and wife, Lotte, committed suicide. He left this farewell note.

"Now I have finished
with all my earthly
business, and high
time, too. Yes, yes,
my dear child,
now comes death."

FRANZ LEHAR

———•◦•———

The son of a composer in the Austro-
Hungarian army, composer Franz Lehar
"stumbled blindly into writing operetta" and
enjoyed his greatest success with *The Merry
Widow.* The operetta was said to have played
simultaneously in five languages in five theaters
in Buenos Aires. He died in 1948 at the age of 78.

"I'm losin'."

FRANCIS ALBERT SINATRA

At the end of a long and tumultuous life during which he won millions of fans and countless accolades, singer, actor, film producer, and bon vivant Frank Sinatra knew when he was licked. It wasn't just the years, but the hours that had dwindled down to a precious few when Old Blue Eyes spoke these last words to his fourth wife, Barbara.

"You sons of bitches, give my love to Mother!"

FRANCIS "TWO-GUN" CROWLEY

Convicted of robbery and murder during the Depression, Crowley issued these hard-boiled instructions while sitting in Sing Sing's electric chair in 1931. Before being taken into custody, Crowley and his girlfriend had held off almost the entire police force of New York City in a West Side brownstone shoot-out.

"Only suckers get hit with right hands."

CHARLIE GOLDMAN

A rguably the best trainer in the history of prizefighting, Goldman had a reputation for being able to transform even the clumsiest of pugilists into champs. His greatest creation was the undefeated heavyweight champ Rocky Marciano. Even at the end, Goldman couldn't resist the opportunity to share his wisdom.

"Some time when
things are going
wrong, when the
breaks are beating
the boys, ask them to
win one for the Gipper.
I don't know where
I'll be then, Rock,
but I'll know about
it and I'll be happy."

GEORGE GIPP

While dying of pneumonia at the height of his fame, Notre Dame football great George Gipp may *not* have made this speech; his coach, Knute Rockne, had a gift for the apocryphal. (Ronald Reagan, who also had a gift for the apocryphal, played Gipp in the 1940 movie *Knute Rockne, All-American*.) But the story goes that eight years after Gipp's death, Rockne urged his troops at half-time of the game with Army to "win one for the Gipper." It worked. Final score: Notre Dame 12, Army 6.

"I deny everything but what I have all along admitted: of a design on my part to free slaves . . . never intended murder or treason or destruction of property, or to incite or excite slaves to rebellion or to make insurrection . . . I believe that to interfere, as I have done, as I have always freely admitted I have done, in behalf of [God's] despised poor, I did not wrong but right . . . Now, if it is deemed necessary that I should forfeit my life for the furthering of the ends of justice, and mingle my blood further with the blood of my children and with the blood of

millions in the slave country
whose rights are disregarded by
wicked, cruel, and unusual
enactments, I say let it be done . . ."

JOHN BROWN

In 1859, the abolitionist John Brown led a group of whites and blacks in a raid at the arsenal in Harper's Ferry, Virgina, in which several people were killed. The state of Virginia convicted Brown of treason, and he became the first American since the nation's founding to be hanged as a traitor. In the North, though, church bells rang in his honor on the day of his execution.

"If it had not been for this thing, I might have lived out my life talking at street corners to scorning men. I might have died unmarked, unknown; a failure. Now we are not a failure. This is our career and our triumph. Never in our full life could we hope to do such work for tolerance, for justice, for man's understanding of man, as now we do by accident. Our words, our lives, our pains: nothing! The taking of our lives, lives of a good shoemaker and a poor fish peddler—all! That last moment belongs to us, that agony is our triumph!"

BARTOLOMEO VANZETTI

I n the Red Scare of 1919–20, two Italian immigrants named Nicola Sacco and Bartolomeo Vanzetti were tried and convicted by the state of Massachussetts for robbing and murdering a paymaster and his guard. They became an international cause célèbre, but their convictions were never overturned and they were executed in 1927. Vanzetti made this statement shortly before death.

"Leave the shower curtain on the inside of the tub."

CONRAD HILTON

Born in San Antonio, New Mexico, Hilton began his career by renting out rooms in his adobe home. He took a job as a local bank cashier, eventually purchased a bank of his own, and later assumed control of a small hotel in Cisco, Texas, in 1919. Over the next sixty years, he built an international hotel empire. On his deathbed in 1979, Hilton was asked if he had any last words of wisdom. He did.

"I have a terrific headache."

FRANKLIN D. ROOSEVELT

While posing for a portrait at his beloved home in Warm Springs, Georgia, in April 1945, FDR complained of a headache to Lucy Page Mercer Rutherford, his long-time mistress, and died soon after of a cerebral hemorrhage. The only four-term U.S. president, the man who lifted America out of the Great Depression left a sorrowful nation behind to confront the last days of World War II.

"I die happy!"

CHARLES JAMES FOX

Fox spent his political life fighting the policies of King George III. He opposed the war to keep the American colonies, supported the French Revolution, and argued to uphold civil liberties during wartime. Though he often lost parliamentary battles, Fox succeeded in abolishing the slave trade in June of 1806, and died exultant a few months later.

"Wait a second."

MADAME DE POMPADOUR

A fortune teller prophesied that the nine-year-old Pompadour (born Jeanne-Antoinette Poisson) would become the mistress to a king. And so she did, becoming mistress to France's Louis XV. While in his court, she sponsored the works of Voltaire and Boucher and brought theatre and art back to the royal court. Never one to appear before a great man looking anything but her best, she put God on hold on her deathbed to apply a final touch of rouge to her cheeks.

"The hearse, the horse, the driver— and enough!"

LUIGI PIRANDELLO

Death came as a relief to Luigi Pirandello, an Italian playwright who specialized in dramas that were a shade on the grotesque side. Given his home life, it's no wonder that Pirandello tended towards pessimism: His wife went mad, and one of his daughters tried to kill herself.

"You can keep the things of bronze and stone and give me one man to remember me just once a year."

DAMON RUNYON

In tabloid reportage and short stories that were made into the musical *Guys and Dolls,* Runyon breathed life into fast-talking New Yorkers. Ironically, the man who made his living with stylized dialogue ("put up your dukes," "monkey business," and "drop dead" were all his) lost his own voice to throat cancer in 1944. He dropped dead of the disease in 1946.

"It has all been very interesting."

LADY MARY WORTLEY MONTAGU

Indeed it had. During the 17th century, when most English women were subjugated at home, the outspoken poet and feminist was traveling the world, having affairs with Italian intellectuals and writing about Turkish bathhouses. There, Lady Montagu learned about the Turkish practice of smallpox inoculation and fought to have it implemented in England when she returned.

"Don't let it end like this. Tell them I said something."

PANCHO VILLA

Mexican revolutionary "Pancho" Villa was "hated by thousands and loved by millions." Born Doroteo Arango, he adopted the name of a dead gang leader after killing his sister's rapist. General "Black Jack" Pershing, one of the many men who pursued him in vain, once told U.S. President Woodrow Wilson, "Villa is everywhere, but Villa is nowhere." Pershing was wrong. When Villa was finally shot to death by his enemies, he was in Chihuahua.

R ay Robinson is a former magazine editor, journalist, and author of many books, including *Iron Horse: Lou Gehrig and His Times* and *Yankee Stadium: 75 Years of Drama, Glamor, and Glory*. He lives in New York City with his wife, Phyllis, and his Norwich terrier, Penelope.